The Thinking Girl's Treasury of Real Princesses

ARTEMISIA OF CARIA

Series editor **Shirin Yim Bridges**
Consulting editor **Amy Novesky**
Copy editor **Jennifer Fry**
Book design **Jay Mladjenovic**

Typeset mainly in Herculanum and Volkswagen TS
Illustrations rendered in pen and watercolor

Manufactured in Singapore

Library of Congress PCN 2010903614

First Edition   10 9 8 7 6 5 4 3 2 1

Goosebottom Books LLC
710 Portofino Lane, Foster City CA 94404

www.goosebottombooks.com

For Tiegan and Alena, the original Thinking Girl
and the real Fairy-Monkey Princess.

~ Shirin Yim Bridges ~

For my family and friends.

~ Albert Nguyen ~

The Thinking Girl's Treasury of Real Princesses

Hatshepsut of Egypt

Artemisia of Caria

Sorghaghtani of Mongolia

Qutlugh Terkan Khatun of Kirman

Isabella of Castile

Nur Jahan of India

ARTEMISIA OF CARIA

By Shirin Yim Bridges | Illustrated by Albert Nguyen

goosebottombooks

She was called what?!

The names in this book can be hard to pronounce, and dictionaries often don't help — trying to work out dictionary pronunciation symbols can be like trying to read Ancient Greek!

Here are most of the unusual names encountered in this book, with a rough-and-easy guide to pronunciation. You can also hear many of these names pronounced on the website www.howjsay.com. Try it, it's neat!

Pliny	plin•nee
Artemisia	ar•tim•mis•sia
Caria	care•ee•ah
Aristotle	air•ris•tot•tel
Gynaikon	guy•nigh•con
Trireme	try•reem
Dido	dye•dough
Hippolyta	hip•pol•lit•tuh
Aegean	ij•gee•en
Xerxes	zerk•sees
Halicarnassus	hal•lee•car•nas•sus
Herodotus	her•rod•dit•is
Thermopylae	ther•mop•pill•lee
Qutlugh	koot•look
Chiton	kite•en
Leonides	lee•on•id•dees

ARTEMISIA 1 OF CARIA

Some people think it very unlucky to have a woman onboard a ship. This superstition, which still exists among some fishermen, is so old that it was first mentioned 2,000 years ago by the ancient historian, Pliny. And this superstition was so strong that in the 14th century, the captain of a ship caught in a storm threw 60 female passengers overboard, thinking that their presence onboard had angered the seas and that their removal would calm the waves. (It did not. The ship was wrecked and the men followed the women to their deaths.)

How surprising, then, that thousands of years ago, in the world of the Ancient Greeks where women were expected to obey their husbands in all matters, to play no part in public life, and to stay inside the house, a princess grew up to be not only a sailor and a ship's captain, but a famous admiral. Her name was Artemisia, and she was the Queen of Caria.

Where she lived

Although the Ancient Greek world is often confusingly referred to as "Ancient Greece," it was not one country but a collection of many separate states on the islands and along the coasts of the Aegean Sea. To add to the confusion, the states west and north of the Aegean at that time are often referred to as "Greece" — so now you have a "Greece" within an "Ancient Greece," and even "Greece" did not have exactly the same borders as those of the modern country, Greece!

Thrace

Macedonia

Phrygia

Epirus

Mystia

Thessaly

Aegean Sea

Lydia

Achaia

Caria

Peloponnesus

Crete

Rh

When she lived

This timeline shows when the other princesses in The Thinking Girl's Treasury of Real Princesses once lived.

1500BC		500BC		1200AD	1300AD	1400AD		1600AD
Hatshepsut of Egypt		Artemisia of Caria		Sorghaghtani of Mongolia	Qutlugh Terkan Khatun	Isabella of Castile		Nur Jahan of India

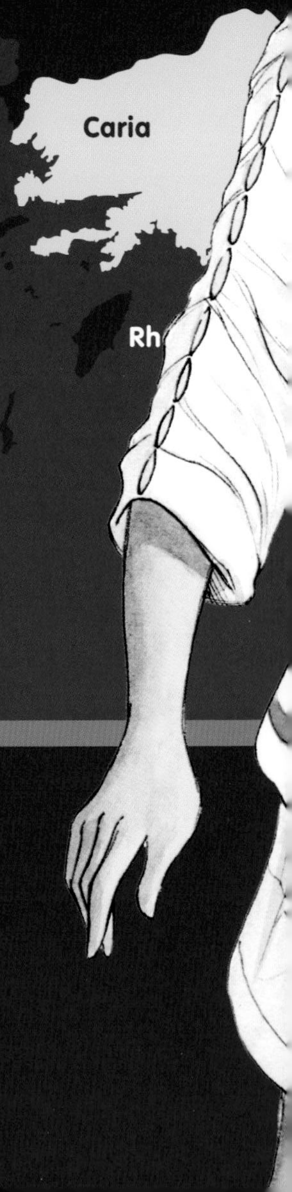

HER STORY

Artemisia was born around 500 BC, in Caria — now the southwest corner of Turkey, but in those days part of Ancient Greece. In the Ancient Greek world, women (even princesses) were less than second-class citizens. In fact, they were not considered citizens at all and had few legal rights. They were not allowed to own property, but were themselves considered the property of a man: a father, brother, or husband. To this man, they were expected to be completely obedient. The great Greek philosopher, Aristotle, voiced the common opinion that a wife's role was to serve her husband even more submissively than if she were a slave bought at the market.

It's not surprising then that most girls were not educated. Despite the fact that half the Greek gods were actually powerful goddesses, Greek women had very limited lives. Girls were kept with their mothers and sisters in the gynaikon, or women's quarters. They were expected to spend most of their time there, weaving cloth and leaving the house only to draw water from the public fountain or to take part in religious festivals.

We don't know anything about Artemisia's life growing up, but it was certainly nothing like the typical life of a girl just described, for somehow Artemisia managed to learn three things:

She learned how to sail triremes, the great warships of Ancient Greece. These were manned by up to 203 sailors. (Artemisia, as you will soon see, became the captain of her own much-feared warship.)

She learned how to fight. Artemisia became not just a captain, but an admiral — a commander of many warships and their captains; and not only an admiral, but the admiral of one of the ancient world's most respected fighting fleets.

She learned how to respect her own opinion, and to speak her own mind. This could not have been easy in a world where nothing a woman said was taken very seriously! But she must have proven herself, because at this time and place in history when women couldn't even inherit their own homes, Artemisia eventually inherited the throne. She became Artemisia I (I means "the First"), ruling Queen of Caria.

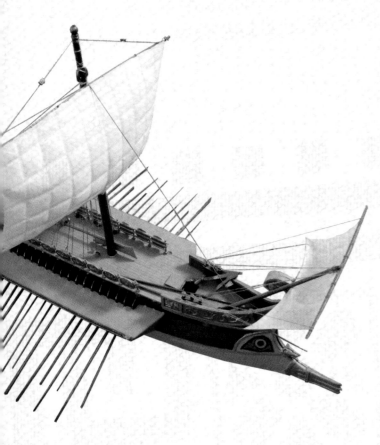

▲ The ships she sailed
The trireme gets its name from its three rows of oars sticking out along both sides of the ship. These were pulled by one oarsmen per oar, sitting in groups of three. Although the trireme also had two sails, these were used mainly to sail to and from battle. During the battle itself, the sails were taken down to give the oarsmen more precise control, allowing tighter turns, sudden changes in direction, etc. In fact, both sails and masts were taken off the ships and left on nearby beaches before the ships went into battle.

We don't know how Artemisia accomplished these things, but we do know that they didn't fall into her lap just because she was a princess. For one thing, no other princess that we know of ever learned how to sail a ship, much less lead a navy. And princesses growing up to rule as queens regnant (queens who ruled by themselves and in their own name) were almost as unheard of. Although the Ancient Greeks had, in addition to their goddesses, mythical queens such as Dido of Carthage and Hippolyta the Amazon, the only other historical queens who reigned in this part of the world and around this time in history were, interestingly enough, two queens of Caria (including an Artemisia II about 100 years after Artemisia I), and Queen Tania of Dardania.

Dido of Carthage

In both Ancient Greek and Roman writings, Dido was the legendary queen and founder of Carthage, a city in what is now Tunisia on the North African coast. She is especially well known for her role in the story of Aeneas, the Trojan hero whose wanderings, in myth, led to the founding of Rome. On his travels, Aeneas spent a year as Dido's lover in Carthage. When he left her, she committed suicide by stabbing herself with his sword and throwing herself onto a burning pyre.

Hippolyta the Amazon

Hippolyta, Queen of the Amazons, was not the proud and warlike character you might expect. She appears a few times in Ancient Greek mythology (most confusingly dying several times). In both the legends of Heracles and Theseus, she welcomes them with gifts when they land on her island. To Heracles, Hippolyta offers her precious girdle. But she is killed in a misunderstanding and Heracles steals that very same girdle! In Theseus' legend, she is rewarded for her generosity by being kidnapped and then abandoned.

What she ate

Four staples of modern Greek food were also staples across the Ancient Greek world: wine, olives, bread, and fish. Wine was not only a popular drink, but an important part of Greek culture, necessary to many religious rituals. Wine production in Europe started in Macedonia, a part of Ancient Greece, more than 6,500 years ago. Olives were a similarly long-established part of the Greek diet. According to legend, the original olive tree grew where the goddess Athena stuck her spear in a rock. That rock was the Acropolis, and around this tree grew the city of Athens.

When Artemisia became Queen of Caria, the eastern states of the Ancient Greek world, including Caria, had already been absorbed into the mighty Persian empire — an empire that stretched to the borders of India in the east, to the southern reaches of Egypt, and to the western tip of Libya. The Persian Great King, Xerxes, was now bent on adding the western and northern states to his domain. (From now on, we will refer to this area that he wanted to conquer as "Greece.") First, he invited the states to join his empire peacefully. "All" they had to do was send him earth and water as a sign that their lands and seas — everything that supported their lives — were now his. So feared was the might of Persia that among the hundreds of Greek city-states, only 31 dared to refuse.

In 480 BC, to the beat of drums and the flap of wind in canvas sails, 72 ships bore out of Halicarnassus harbor (the main city of Caria). Leading them with an elite squadron of five ships under her personal command was Artemisia, standing at the helm, her linen robe pressed against her body by the wind, her eyes narrowed against the sparkle of the Aegean Sea. Below her, 174 men bent their backs and strained against their oars, adding their power to that of the sails. Artemisia and her fleet had been summoned to join Xerxes, who was assembling the largest fighting force the world had ever seen, for the sole purpose of beating the 31 defiant Greek states into submission.

At Xerxes' command was an army of maybe 150,000 soldiers, a navy of more than 1,200 ships and 250,000 sailors, as well as the kings of many countries within his empire. (These numbers are only scholars' guesses. The ancient historian, Herodotus, claimed that Xerxes had more than one million men!) Whatever the exact numbers, this army was so large that it was said to drink the rivers dry; its arrows were said to darken the skies and its ships to blacken the seas. And among all these men, Artemisia was the only woman. In fact, the Greeks were so offended that a woman was actually taking up arms against them that they offered a special 10,000 drachmae reward for her head.

What she wore

Clothing was quite similar throughout the Ancient Greek world. The main garment for women was a long tunic, called the chiton. This varied from country to country only in its fabric — linen or wool — and in the details of how it was buckled or fastened together.

Belt or ribbon, known as the *girdle*. When two were worn, one slightly above the other as shown, it was known as a *double girdle*.

Long tunic or *chiton*. In Caria, these were made of linen, although wool was used in other parts of Ancient Greece.

When women needed their legs free to be able to run or jump — as Artemisia surely would have in the thick of a battle — they simply shortened their chitons by pulling the fabric through the middle of their double girdle, letting the extra cloth hang over in a fold.

But when this great force finally clashed with the Greeks, it wasn't the complete rout that everyone had expected. At the land battle of Thermopylae, the immense Persian army struggled to overwhelm a mere 7,000 men. The sea battle was even less of a success. A storm destroyed as much as a third of the Persian fleet but left the Greek ships mostly untouched. Xerxes was furious. With his army, he had burned the city of Athens, but he didn't feel that this made up for the 400 Persian ships that had been sunk. Xerxes was what you might call a sore loser. Also, you could say he had a big head. He was sure that his navy had lost because he had not been there in person. Next time, he thought, he would set his throne high on a cliff and intimidate his navy into smashing the Greeks to smithereens.

A legendary last stand

Thermopylae was the site of the legendary stand of King Leonides and his 300 Spartans. Defending a narrow pass through the mountains, these 301 men with another 7,000 Greeks from various cities held back the Persian army of hundreds of thousands for days. They were not defeated until a traitor showed the Persians a secret path that would allow them to attack the Greeks simultaneously from behind. When the Spartans heard that they had been betrayed, they sent the other Greeks home to fight another day. They then held the pass for as long as they could, protecting the body of their king when he fell, and dying to the last man.

That night, on the sands before the drawn-up fleet and to the sawing and hammering of hasty repairs, Xerxes put this plan to all his commanders. They knew full well what Xerxes wanted them to say, so they all agreed that it was a great idea. All except Artemisia. She had fought well and bravely that day, but the men were still surprised to hear her raise her voice among them.

Measuring her words, Artemisia said: "Great King, here's my true opinion. Do not fight this sea battle. You already have Athens, and all the rest of Greece. If you advance now on land, you will scatter the Greeks before you. But if you stay to fight again at sea, you may lose your fleet, and this would in turn do your army great harm."

There's another story about Xerxes' big head. On his way to Greece, a storm blew up and wrecked a bridge he was about to cross. Xerxes was so furious that he had the waves whipped! He obviously thought they should answer to the Great King of Persia.

You could have heard a pin drop. Artemisia's allies among her fellow captains were afraid that she had angered Xerxes by daring to disagree. Those who thought that a woman had no place among them were pleased. With smirks on their faces they turned to Xerxes, hoping to witness the royal temper.

But Xerxes simply thanked Artemisia for her opinion. He was still intent on destroying the Greek fleet, and he was sure of his success, so he moved on to planning another sea battle.

The Battle of Salamis, which Xerxes watched from his throne on a cliff, roaring in frustration, was a complete disaster. Nearly all of the Persian fleet were destroyed. As Xerxes watched, the waters below him became littered with the flotsam of broken ships and the bodies of drowned men. In the chaos and confusion, he saw Artemisia's ship being chased by an enemy. Daringly, it rammed and sank a ship that was in its way, breaking free. "Ah!" exclaimed Xerxes, "My men have become women, and my women men!"

GREECE
SKODRA
Black Sea
SALAMIS
SARDES
CAPPADOCIA
ARMENIA
Caspian Sea
Oxus River
CYPRUS
Mediterranean Sea
ASSYRIA
Euphrates River
Tigris River
BABYLONIA
ELAM
MEDIA
HYRCANIA
PARTHIA
ARIA
LYBIA
ARABIA
SAGARTIA
PERSIA
DRANGIA
EGYPT
Nile River
Persian Gulf
M A K A

Egyptian ships
Corinthian ships
Throne of Xerxes
X
Salamis
Persian main force
Greek main force

Where she fought

Everything in white was part of Xerxes' empire. You can see why he got such a big head. You can also see why he thought Greece was the next bit of land he should add to his domain. The naval battle where Artemisia became famous was fought off the island of Salamis. The spot where Xerxes watched from his throne is shown by an x on the map.

In the aftermath of this terrible defeat, Artemisia found herself summoned to speak to Xerxes in private. She was now the only person he trusted to give him both honest and sage advice. What should he do next, the Great King asked?

Her advice was once again honest and practical. Artemisia counseled Xerxes to take most of his troops home, leaving some to try to finish off the Greeks under the command of his best general. If a final attack was successful and the Greeks were completely defeated, Greece would become part of Xerxes' empire. But if the Greeks won, they would not win much, for Xerxes would be safe at home on his throne, in a position to attack them again.

So, Xerxes went back to Persia with most of his army. (He never did manage to annex all of Greece.) He marked his trust in Artemisia by making her the guardian of his sons on their journey home (for they had come to watch the war in the same way that you might go to watch a game of football). For being the only person brave enough to give Xerxes honest advice, Artemisia may have received a gift: in the British Museum is a precious calcite jar that was found in Caria. It bears the signature of the Great King Xerxes, and it's believed to have been a personal present from Xerxes to Artemisia I — princess, admiral, and Queen of Caria.

THE NOT-SO-NICE PART OF HER STORY

At the Battle of Salamis, Artemisia found herself trapped by a wall of ships. She could have turned to fight, but turning would have slowed her down and speed was critical. Mounted below the prow at the waterline, ships carried huge battering rams. But for ramming to be successful, a ship had to be moving quickly.

Instead of turning, Artemisia ordered her men to propel her ship full speed ahead, ramming straight into the side of the ship that was in her way, splintering and cutting through it, and sinking it with all hands on deck (that means every sailor onboard was drowned). Plowing through the wreckage, she sailed her own ship to freedom.

This bold attack lead to Xerxes' famous comment and won his lasting admiration. However, there was one thing that Xerxes did not know, and which the drowned men couldn't tell him. The ship that Artemisia sank was not an enemy ship. It was one of Xerxes' own.

How honest and courageous had Artemisia been to sink a ship on her own side? Was she a coward saving her own skin? Or was she protecting the lives of her men, at the cost of the lives of others? Only one thing is clear. It's difficult and very rare to be completely praiseworthy. (Some princesses did manage it. But more on that in the book about Qutlugh Terkan Khatun of Kirman.)